PEACE

AND JUSTICE

MINISTRY:

A Practical Guide

HOW TO START A PEACE AND JUSTICE GROUP

IN YOUR LOCAL CHURCH OR

MAKE AN EXISTING ONE MORE EFFECTIVE

Richard K. Taylor

🌳 **BROWN-ROA**
A Division of Wm. C. Brown Communications, Inc.
Dubuque, Iowa

Book Team

Publisher—Ernest T. Nedder
Managing Editor—Mary Jo Graham
Assistant Editor—Sharon Cruse
Production Manager—Marilyn Rothenberger
Art Director—Cathy Frantz
Illustrator—Jim Ehlinger

Scripture Sources

The New American Bible with Revised New Testament,
copyright © 1986 by The Confraternity of Christian
Doctrine, Washington, D.C. Published by Benziger
Publishing Company, Mission Hills, CA.

ISBN 0–697–17798–X

10 9 8 7 6 5 4 3 2 1

Contents

Introduction _____ v

Chapter One _____ 1
What is a Peace and Justice Ministry?

Chapter Two _____ 17
How to Start a Peace and Justice Ministry
in Your Local Church

Chapter Three _____ 27
Helping Your Peace and Justice Ministry Grow

Chapter Four _____ 51
How Your Group Can Work for Peace and Justice

Appendix 1 _____ 75
Resources for Study, Worship, Reflection and Training

Appendix 2 _____ 83
National Peace, Justice and Ecology Organizations

Acknowledgements

I want to express my appreciation to Dale Mezzacappa (journalist), Sue Rardin (novelist), and Jeaneen Riely (nurturer of parish peace and justice groups) for their many helpful suggestions on this book as it was in process. I also want to thank Sister Marion Dillon for her encouragement to me to write a book on parish peace and justice ministries. Most of all, I want to express my gratitude and love to my wife, Phyllis, not only for her support for my writing, but for the inspiration of the most compassionate heart I have ever known.

Introduction

This is a practical book about how to form a peace and justice group in your local parish or congregation. Its four concise chapters describe:

- the key characteristics of a peace and justice ministry and the issues it might address;
- how to organize such a ministry in your local church;
- how to nurture the group, focusing on such issues as selecting leadership, resolving conflicts, setting goals and priorities, holding effective meetings and evaluating the group's efforts;
- how to develop significant, worthwhile programs.

The appendices provide lists of peace and justice resources, study suggestions and worship ideas. All of this material is based on my experience in starting a peace and justice group in my local Catholic parish, St. Vincent de Paul, and in helping to start similar parish-based groups through the Commission for World Peace and Justice of the Archdiocese of Philadelphia.

Because of this experience, you may note a certain Catholic "angle" in some of the pages that follow. However, I grew up as a Quaker and have worked closely all my life with people of many faiths around common concerns. These relationships also have influenced my writing. Therefore, I hope that people of many backgrounds—not just Catholics—will find this manual helpful in their efforts to be peacemakers and justice-seekers.

The rest of the book is a practical guide. Here, let me tell you *why* I believe Christians are called to work for justice and peace, especially in their local churches.

Jesus once told the story of a rich man who ignored a very poor man named Lazarus living at his gate. Lazarus gladly would have licked the crumbs from the rich man's plate, but the rich man gave him nothing. When they died, Lazarus was carried by the angels to heaven, but the rich man went to the torment of Hades (Luke 16:19–31).

This parable shows how seriously Jesus takes our obligation to help the poor and needy. To ignore human suffering, Jesus teaches, is radical evil. It was the rich man's indifference to Lazarus that sent him to hell. Jesus is telling us that we must not be apathetic in the face of relievable human suffering.

The Bible is full of similar teaching. The Bible depicts God as indignant over the plight of the poor and passionately concerned about social justice. God commands us to correct unjust and oppressive social conditions that create poverty and misery. The Bible even questions whether or not we can really be the people of God if we

vi

neglect the poor and don't work to free the oppressed.[1]

Scripture does not teach, however, that work for justice must be hard, laborious duty. On the contrary, it promises rich blessings for the just and compassionate. For the Bible, fighting against injustice is a way to be happy, healed, and close to God. The prophet Isaiah, for example, assures us that our wounds will quickly heal, that our gloom and darkness will be dispelled and that God will guide us and answer our prayers if we set free the oppressed, shelter the homeless, clothe the naked, and feed the hungry (Isaiah 58:6–11).

Jesus is equally clear that those who respond compassionately to human suffering will be blessed. "Come, you who are blessed by my Father," he says invitingly. "Inherit the kingdom prepared for you from the foundation of the world. For I was hungry and you gave me food, I was thirsty and you gave me drink, a stranger and you welcomed me, naked and you clothed me, ill and you cared for me, in prison and you visited me." When the righteous express surprise at such blessing, he tells them with great love that whatever they did for the least, they did for him. (Matthew 25:34–40)

Those who respond to simple human need, therefore, will meet Christ himself. To act justly

---

[1] For example, God's indignation over the suffering of the poor is portrayed vividly in Proverbs 14:31, Isaiah 3:14–15, and Amos 2:6–7. Psalms 146:7–9 and Isaiah 10:1–4 are two places among many where we hear God's passion for social justice. See Appendix 1 for a Scripture study that shows God's deep fervor about social justice and God's call to us to show the same deep-felt concern.

and mercifully is to live most truly, for such action reflects the very nature of God and expresses the image of God within us. It is a path by which we may know God in the deepest possible way.

Jesus also promises rich blessings to those who work for peace. "Blessed are the peacemakers, for they will be called children of God" (Matthew 5:9). The God of the Bible is "the God of peace." When "the God of love and peace" (2 Corinthians 13:11) is with us, we want to live in peace with one another and to help bring peace to our war-ravaged world.[2]

Given this pervasive Scriptural teaching, it is no wonder that the church throughout the ages has spoken out frequently for justice and peace. Recently, the U.S. Catholic bishops said in their pastoral letter on peace: "Peacemaking is not an optional commitment. It is a requirement of our faith. We are called to be peacemakers, not by some movement of the moment, but by our Lord Jesus Christ."[3] Three years later, their pastoral letter on economic justice stated: "The life and words of Jesus and the teaching of his church call us to serve those in need and to work actively for social and economic justice."[4]

---

[2] God is referred to as "the God of peace" in Romans 15:33, Philippians 4:9, 1 Thessalonians 5:23 and Hebrews 13:20.

[3] *The Challenge of Peace: God's Promise and Our Response,* (Washington, DC: *Origins,* May 19, 1983), page 30.

[4] *Economic Justice for All: Catholic Social Teaching and the U.S. Economy* (Washington, DC: *Origins,* November 27, 1986), page 410.

viii

Other churches have made similar statements. Thus, if we accept the teaching of Scripture and of the church, we must see that Christians are called to work for justice and peace.

For most of us, this is a hard call to accept directly and personally. However, its clarity and its promise are undeniable and compelling. They are the reason you are holding this book in your hands today.

The good news is that the Bible pledges that we have Divine companionship in our struggle for peace and justice. God's call is high, but if we seek prayerfully to follow Jesus Christ, God's love can make us what that love has called us to be.

How can we, with God's help, express this common calling? Clearly, we must live out our discipleship as individuals, as members of families, in our work, our neighborhoods and in our public life as citizens. This book, however, focuses on how we carry out Christ's mandate as members of parishes and congregations, that is, as the body of Christ.

St. Paul speaks repeatedly of the church as "the body of Christ." "So we, though many, are one body in Christ and individually parts of one another" (Romans 12:5). Christ's followers are not meant to live and work alone. Jesus prayed that we would know a profound oneness, not only with him, but with each other (John 17:20–23). We make up a living community, the body whose head is Jesus Christ.

As we come together in worship, we pray

that this body be transformed more and more into the image of Christ, the head. In the words of a popular Communion song:

> To be your bread now, be your wine now, Lord, come and change us, to be a sign of your love.
> Blessed and broken, poured and flowing, gift that you gave us,
> to be your body once again.[5]

Eucharist is love broken and given, love poured out and flowing. We are to be that bread, that wine, that love for others. Eucharist calls us to "break" ourselves, as Christ did, in the service of others. We are to be Christ's body once again.

How can we be that body, acting for peace and justice? How can we employ our many gifts to be peacemakers and justice-seekers?

Back in 1981 we asked this question at my local parish, St. Vincent de Paul in Philadelphia. After much prayer and discussion, we came together to form what we called a Parish Peace Ministry. One of our first projects was the delightful one of entertaining thirty Buddhist monks who were walking on a peace pilgrimage across the world. A month later, we arranged transportation so that parishioners could join 750,000 others at a peace rally at the United Nations, followed by a profoundly moving peace Mass at a local Catholic Church. For over a

[5] *To Be Your Bread,* written by David Hass, Copyright 1981–82, all rights reserved, published by Cooperative Ministries, Inc. Used with permission in *Today's Missal: Music Issue 1991* (Portland, OR: Oregon Catholic Press, Vol. 58, No. 1, 1991), song number 393.

dozen years now, our Peace Ministry has been a vital part of the life of our parish, using films, discussions, written materials and workshops to educate all of us about peace and justice issues and helping us respond to these issues in our city, nation and world.

Some years after we began, the Arch-diocesan Commission for Peace and Justice adopted as a goal the creation of peace and justice groups in Philadelphia's parishes. When they began this work, only about a dozen such groups existed. Now we have ninety, covering nearly a third of the parishes in the Archdiocese. New groups are formed regularly. Some struggle hard and feel frustrated and unappreciated. Others have been well received in their parishes and have done important work in education and action.

The first edition of this manual was written to help groups in Philadelphia and other parts of the country get organized and develop effective work. Every copy was sold, making necessary this new, updated and completely revised edition.

Imagine if every American parish, congregation, and local Church had a trained and effective group striving to live out the biblical call to struggle for justice and peace. God's passion for peace and justice would be expressed, not just by a few religious leaders in their occasional statements or by a few national organizations and their limited membership, but in every city and town and village across this land. Congregations would not be just "houses of worship," but places where people of faith are living out God's call to "make justice your aim" (Isaiah 1:16). The oppressed and the forgotten would find new allies in their struggle for liberation. The church—the Body of Christ of which we are members—would more nearly live out the words of St. John, "Let us not love in word or speech but in deed and truth" (1 John. 3:18).

This manual is dedicated to the development and nurture of these groups. It seeks to support people of faith who believe with St. James that "faith of itself, if it does not have works, is dead" (James. 2:17).

Chapter One

What is a Peace and Justice Ministry?

A *Peace and Justice Ministry* is a group of Christians in a local church who work together for peace and justice.[6] Living in a world torn by war, hatred, oppression, racism, poverty, ecological destruction and other evils, we want Jesus' prayer, "Your kingdom come, your will be done, on earth as in heaven," to be more than words on our lips. We know that God's kingdom will come in its fullness only by God's action. But, with Christ's help, we want to do our part to make this earth *more like* that kingdom. We've caught a vision of a world where the sacred human dignity of every person is respected, where justice is more the norm, where the earth is being freed from the torment of war, where people are learning to live in harmony with the environment and where all are moving toward full equality of opportunity and of responsibility.

Spread across the country and the world in a great variety of congregations, we are very diverse. We don't fit any mold. But the following are some qualities that many of us share and that give us our special character as peace and justice ministries.

For example, most of us see the vital importance of feeding the hungry, clothing the naked and otherwise directly helping those in need. But we also ask, "*Why* are so many of God's children hungry, or ill-housed, or dressed

---

[6] Using the exact name "Peace and Justice Ministry" is not important. In some churches, the group may be called a "Social Concerns Group," a "Social Action Committee," a "Peace Mission Group" or some other name. The title "peace and justice ministry" has the advantages of emphasizing the group's "service" role. The important thing, however, is what the group does, not what it is called.

3

in rags, or at war?" We want to address the *roots* of social problems, not just the fruits. We hear God's call, not only to be charitable, but to work for social justice.[7]

Benedictine Sister Joan Chittister tells the story of "Big Boulder" to show the difference between charity and justice. It seems that a massive boulder had fallen into the middle of a highway. Cars would zip around the curve and crash into it. A family living nearby was horrified and moved to pity by the sight. They would help people from their smashed-up cars, tend their injuries, feed them, pray with them and send them on their way. Finally, after years of compassionate care, one family member said, "You know, we really should try to move that boulder."

Members of Peace and Justice Ministries want to move boulders as well as care for hurting people. We know that the poor can be harmed by individual acts of cruelty or indifference, as in the parable of Lazarus and the rich man. But we are challenged by the realization that many more are

---

[7] "Charity" has to do with our personal, practical response of mercy and compassion toward those who are in need, e.g., organizing a soup kitchen to feed the hungry. "Justice" is more concerned with shaping society's legal, political and economic systems to make them more supportive of human dignity, e.g., passing legislation to fund programs to eliminate hunger and malnutrition throughout the society.

The Bible does not seek to define the word "justice" philosophically so much as to express God's passion for justice, God's abhorrence of injustice and our obligation as God's children to be just. The Bible tells us more of the **heart** than of the mind of God. However, a **definition** of justice drawn from biblical faith might be: A standard by which the benefits and penalties of living in society are distributed in order to uphold fairness and the equal human dignity of all persons, especially the poor and vulnerable, in social, economic and political relationships.

4

damaged by laws and social policies that fail to provide the poor with adequate housing, education, medical care and other supports for their human dignity. *Nations* can act like the rich man and Lazarus. Therefore, we reach for a society that—in its laws, its policies, its institutions, its leadership—will treat its most vulnerable citizens as made in the image of God. We want to act justly in our personal, one-to-one relationships, but we also try to remember the prophet's call to change "unjust statutes" and "oppressive decrees" that deprive the needy of justice, "robbing my people's poor of their rights" (Isaiah 10:1–2).

We want everyone—from whatever background—to be treated fairly and justly. But we remember Christ's special concern for the poor. Therefore, we not only try to aid the poor, but we wrestle with how to help empower them and how to stand in solidarity with them in the struggle for justice.

We try to keep in mind the intimate relationship between justice and peace.[8] We remember Isaiah's profound insight that "justice will bring about peace; right will produce calm and serenity" (Isaiah 32:17). We want to be peacemakers in our personal relationships. But we

---

[8] Just as with the word "justice," the Bible holds no philosophical definition of "peace." As used in the Bible, the word "peace" has an extremely rich meaning. In the Hebrew word **shalom**, it refers to wholeness or well-being. The Greek word, used in the New Testament, normally describes the absence of war or conflict. A definition of peace drawn from biblical faith might be: The absence of strife, vengeance or bloodshed between individuals, groups or nations, rooted in a commitment to justice and respect for human dignity.

5

also do what we can to support peaceful ways of resolving conflict and nonviolent methods of working for change in the local, national and even the international scene. We are inspired by a vision of a world like the one the Psalmist saw when he sang, "Kindness and truth shall meet; justice and peace shall kiss" (Psalms 85:11).

Paul VI - put

Seven Key Characteristics of a Peace and Justice Ministry

1. Ministry

The term "to minister" means "to serve." It reminds us that one of our main purposes is to serve the Christian community. Our role is not to criticize or judge other members of the parish. We must avoid the temptation to feel superior or "farther along" because of our commitment to peace and justice. Rather, we should look for ways to help fellow Christians on their journey so that they too can hear God's call to be peacemakers and justice-seekers. We must be prophetic without being arrogant.

We can minister in the faith that the Holy Spirit is already at work in our local congregation. Christ's Spirit is drawing people to "make justice your aim" (Isaiah 1:17) and to "live at peace with all" (Romans 12:18). We cooperate with the Spirit when we help this to happen. Together, all of us in the local Church are the community of Christ's disciples. Together we can find the peacemaking and justice-seeking tasks to which Christ uniquely calls each of us. This can be an exciting adventure of discovery, rather than a burden weighing us down.

2. Persistence

We must be realistic about the difficulty of bringing our concerns to the parish and the community. Many Christian brothers and sisters are not familiar with the social teachings of the Church. They may even oppose our efforts as "too controversial" or "not having anything to do with religion." In some parishes, ironically, "peace" and "justice" are fighting words![9] Also, work with the poor and efforts to bring about social change are not always easy. All of these difficulties, however, can be a challenge to our creativity and resourcefulness. We may even find ourselves saying humorously to one another, "Wow, what great training this is giving us in how to be loving, nonviolent peacemakers in the face of opposition!"

3. Prayerfulness

A big temptation in working for peace and justice is to become so concerned with issues and actions and programs that we forget the spiritual roots of our witness. This is a prescription for

---

[9] Dom Helder Camara, a Brazilian Catholic Bishop who has suffered much for his work on behalf of the poor and human rights, found this out when he challenged injustice in his society. "When I fed the hungry," he commented, "they called me a saint; but when I asked, 'Why are they hungry?' they called me a communist."

burnout. We need to remind ourselves that the source of our work is Christ's gift: "Peace I leave with you; my peace I give to you; not as the world gives do I give to you" (John 14:27). Prayer opens us to receive this gift. Therefore, we need to pray individually and as a group. We'll be most open to the Spirit if we, like Jesus, take regular time for prayer, spiritual retreat and on-going conversation with God. We are not secular peace activists but followers of Christ who are trying to be channels of God's passion for justice and peace.

4. Friendship

Because the issues of peace and justice are so urgent and often so heart-rending, it's tempting to let our meetings be completely taken up with pressing business. But if we serve the God of love, then it's important to remember the call to express that love to one another. Our "business" shouldn't exclude our "bondedness." Therefore, time can be set aside in meetings for personal sharing so that we become acquainted on more than one dimension. Outside meetings, we can strengthen our friendship through picnics, potlucks, parties, retreats, sports or just getting together to talk.

5. Reconciliation

Peacemaking and justice-seeking will not be authentic unless members of a Peace and

Justice Ministry are at peace with one another. We have no greater peace or justice to give to the world than the quality of peace and mutual respect we experience in our Christian fellowship. We dare not forget St. Paul's words, "Love one another with mutual affection" (Romans 12:10). This means having patience with each other, trusting and forgiving, working out problems and conflicts. It does not mean that we never have disagreements or discord. Far from it! It does mean that we try to resolve them and learn from them. It does mean that we try to remove violence and injustice from our own hearts and lives as well as from the world.

6. Education

The issues with which the ministries deal are complex. Therefore, we're challenged to spend time in self-education and in sharing information with one another and with other members of the congregation. We can take advantage of well-informed speakers, study guides, books, magazines, films, videos and other resources that can help us become better informed. We can join local and national peace and justice organizations whose publications provide both information and inspiration.[10]

---

[10] See Appendix 2 for a description of some experienced, reliable peace, justice, and ecology organizations.

7. Action

Education is vital, but equally important is not getting bogged down in what Martin Luther King, Jr. called "the paralysis of analysis." We hear the call, therefore, to engage in a wide variety of actions, both on our own initiative and in cooperation with others. Action can be controversial, but faith, by its very nature, demands action. "Faith of itself, if it does not have works, is dead" (James 2:17).

Issues that a Peace and Justice Ministry Might Address

A peace and justice issue emerges anywhere that God's will for peace and justice on earth is not being done. Therefore, the issues on which a Peace and Justice Ministry might take action are superabundant. In Chapter 3, we'll discuss how to discern *which* issues your own ministry might take up. For now, let's note just a few of the many issues that a Peace and Justice Ministry might address.

• *Poverty:* How not only to help the poor, but to stand with them in the struggle for justice and to create a society where the weakest among us have first claim on our efforts and priorities.

• *Affordable Housing:* How to ensure that everyone, especially the poor, live in housing that supports their human dignity.

10

• *Homelessness:* How to respond compassionately to the homeless in our midst and to work for a society in which no one will have to live on the streets.

• *Unemployment:* How to help the jobless find work while at the same time lobbying for public policies to assure that all those who can work are able to do so.

• *Health Care Reform:* How to respond compassionately to the sick while striving for a system that guarantees access to high quality, comprehensive, affordable health care for all people without regard to health status, employment or income.

• *Racism:* How to form alliances between majority and minority group people in the struggle for justice while building a society where people will be judged by the content of their character rather than the color of their skins.

• *Ecology:* How to be ecologically responsible as individuals, families and congregations while working for public policies that support conservation, recycling, clean air and water, alternative energy and other ecologically-sound measures.

• *Human Rights:* How to work effectively to free political prisoners unjustly jailed and often tortured in so many countries around the world and to create structures that prevent such unjust imprisonment.

● *War and Peace:* How to contribute to the peaceful resolution of conflict in one's neighborhood, city, nation and world and to find creative nonviolent substitutes for violence.

● *Military Spending and Disarmament:* How to responsibly reduce military spending, channel the funds to meet civilian needs and provide jobs for those unemployed by military budget cut-backs.

● *International Injustice:* How to support people fleeing persecution while challenging powerful governments (including our own) when they use their power to try to dominate, control and exploit weaker countries.

● *World Hunger:* How to eliminate hunger, not just by supporting soup kitchens or donating food or money for relief, but by changing government policies and priorities so that we'll no longer have 450 million people in the world malnourished or facing starvation.

Some other important issues that a peace and justice group might work on are: capital punishment, prison reform, abortion, sexism and women's rights, rights of the mentally ill, support for families and children, tax reform, domestic violence, mistreatment of the elderly, the impaired and the disabled, working conditions and workers' rights, violence in the mass media, war toys, discrimination against homosexuals, welfare reform, urban violence and gun control, neighborhood development, political corruption, substance abuse, crime, reform of the justice system, education, violence in schools, church renewal, agriculture policy, affluent lifestyles, exploitation of farm workers, long-standing conflicts (as in the Middle East, Northern Ireland and South Africa), international trade policy, peace and justice in Central America, nonviolent conflict resolution, refugees and immigration policy, international arms sales, foreign policy and foreign aid, ending the testing of nuclear weapons. I'm sure you could add other important issues to the list.

How a Peace and Justice Ministry Develops

Peace and Justice Ministries do not come into being or develop according to one single pattern. Their growth depends on who is involved, their backgrounds, their knowledge of the issues, the support or opposition they encounter, and so forth. But certain basics almost always occur:

1. A small group of people in a local Church gather to pray, share and learn about peace and justice issues and their responsibility as Christians.

2. They are motivated to continue because they find what they do educational, challenging, satisfying and expressive of their faith.

3. The congregation's minister or priest becomes involved, at least to the extent of being supportive of the group. Parish peace groups can develop without this clergy support, but lack of it means that the group will find it harder to bring its concerns into the heart of parish life.

4. The group develops a clear sense of purpose and goals, often expressing this in a written mission statement. It develops a sense of calling around certain specific peace and justice issues and becomes well informed about these.

5. The group does a lot of education in the parish around the specific issues it has chosen, keeping to the fore the religious dimension of their concern. They distribute literature and bring in speakers, films and other resources. They do not judge or berate other members of the Church, but instead see themselves as "servants" who are trying to help nourish and encourage the peace gifts that the Holy Spirit has placed in each member.

6. The ministry organizes some actions or programs around its peace and justice concerns and draws in other members of the congregation.

7. A broader circle of Church members become interested in the issues and express this by joining the ministry or by supporting its work.

8. Once the ministry is secure in its own existence, it reaches out to other congregations or peace and justice groups to work cooperatively in common efforts.

Chapter Two

How to Start a Peace

and Justice Ministry

in Your Local Church

Here is a step-by-step approach for starting a peace and justice ministry in your local congregation. It is written in "one, two, three" order, but probably the real-life situation in your local Church will not be so neat. So just use the following as a general guideline.

Step 1

Look at Your Own Calling and Motivation

Why do you want to start a Peace and Justice Ministry in your Church? Have you prayed about this? Is the Lord's Spirit inviting you to initiate this work? Do you have gifts to start such a group? Can you imagine this involvement giving you joy and peace? Can you deal with the inevitable pain that comes with trying to respond compassionately to human suffering? Why do you believe your local Church has the potential for starting such a ministry? Can you deal with the fact that some people won't be interested—or may even oppose your effort?

You also should ask some practical questions. Do you have the *time* to take this on, given that it probably will involve *at least* one more meeting per month? Are there other, less important commitments that you could drop to free time for this? Do you enjoy working in collaborative efforts with others? Do you have some initial ideas for what a group like this could do? Are there certain peace and justice issues about which you feel particularly strongly and would like the group to address?

If you have positive answers to most of these questions, then you're probably ready to take the next step of inviting others to join you.

Step 2

Identify Interested People

A Peace and Justice Ministry begins when a group of people in a congregation become interested and start meeting together. No need for a big group.

> Jesus said, "Where two or three are gathered together in my name, there I am in the midst of them" (Matthew 18:20).

Many effective parish-based peace and justice groups started with only two or three interested people. So don't worry if at first you can't think of many people who would join the group. If your effort is rooted in the Lord, it will bear fruit, whether the group is big or small.

How can you locate potentially interested people? Here are ten suggestions:

1. Develop a relationship of trust with your minister/priest. Explain why you want to start a peace and justice ministry. Make clear this is your faith response, not just a political activity.

20

See if your pastor will support your effort and suggest people who might be interested. (Sadly, some pastors are unsupportive, in spite of the clear message of the Bible and the Church's social teachings about peace and justice. In such cases, great tact and wisdom are required to find ways to move forward in spite of this lack of support.)

2. Talk to members of your Church's governing or advisory bodies—the pastoral team, parish council, vestry, session, etc. Ask them who they think might be interested in a local peace and justice group.

3. Think about your own friends and acquaintances from the Church. Who has expressed interest in social issues or seemed concerned about human suffering, injustice, violence or war?

4. Does your Church have a staff person who specializes in social concerns, e.g., a Parish Social Minister? He or she may be working with people who would be interested.

5. Does your Church already have groups that work on social concerns—a Pro-Life Group, a ministry to the homeless, a Social Action Committee, a race relations group? Some of the members might be interested in your ideas.

6. Does your denomination, conference or diocese have a social concerns or peace program? Perhaps a staff or committee person there will know someone in your local Church who is on their mailing list or who has attended one of their events.

7. Don't ignore people who are concerned about patriotism and good citizenship. Make peace and justice a good citizenship issue that will attract their involvement. And remember new people joining your church. Greet them warmly, take an interest in them, and ask them if they would like to be involved.

8. Try writing a brief, one or two-page description of your own concept of a peace and justice ministry. Circulate it in your Church and ask those interested to respond.

9. If your Church has a newsletter or parish bulletin, put a note in it explaining your ideas and inviting people to a meeting.

10. Ask for five minutes at the close of Sunday worship to state your plans, inviting those interested to meet you afterwards. Or get your pastor's support and ask him or her to make the announcement.

Step 3

Call a Meeting and Invite Interested People

Decide first what kind of meeting you want. Would the people you are inviting respond best to an inspirational meeting with a good speaker, a thought-provoking film or a video? Or would the invitees prefer an informal meeting, perhaps in someone's home, where you can discuss the idea among yourselves?

In any case, invite the potentially interested people. You'll get the best response if you contact as many people as possible personally or by phone. However, it's also effective to send out mailings, put up posters, distribute flyers, and put a notice in the parish bulletin. Ask your minister to announce the meeting from the pulpit and to lend support. Ask parish groups to announce the event at their meetings. With your minister's support, you might even be able to send a letter of invitation to the whole congregation's mailing list. Give people at least a couple of weeks' to a month's notice so they're less likely to have conflicting commitments.

Step 4

Prepare for the Meeting

Make arrangements for the location. If you are having the inspirational kind of meeting, invite the speaker well ahead of time and get the equipment necessary for the film or video. In either type of meeting, give some thought in advance to what you want to say and how to gauge people's interest in starting a group. Also, plan a good group process for the meeting (see Step 5) so that people will share honestly and fully. Prepare refreshments. You may want to have some literature available from a local or national peace and justice group for people to take home with them. If you've written up your own ideas, be sure to have copies available for everyone.

Step 5

Hold the Meeting

Prepare your refreshments and put out your literature ahead of time. If you're having a film or video, set up the equipment and test it well before the meeting begins. Here are some suggestions for the first meeting:

1. Open with prayer.

2. Have people introduce themselves, telling who they are and why they came to the meeting.

3. Explain your own concerns—why you called the meeting, why you think it's important to start a group, any ideas you have for its focus and how it could be gotten off the ground. (Don't take too much time—long enough to express your concerns clearly, but not so long as to dominate the meeting. Encourage others to give their ideas.)

4. General discussion. What do others think?

5. Commitment. Who would like to meet again to start work on organizing a peace and justice ministry? Have a sign-up sheet and get the names, addresses and phone numbers of those interested. Ask if one or two people would like to work with you to help plan the next get-together.

6. Set a date, place and time for the next meeting.

7. Closing prayer.

8. Refreshments and informal discussion.

Chapter Three

Helping Your Peace and

Justice Ministry Grow

Let's assume you've had your first meeting and that a group has expressed interest in forming a Peace and Justice Ministry. What do you do next? What problems may crop up? How can you take the next steps in organizing so that the group will develop meaningfully? Here are some ideas drawn from the experience of existing Peace and Justice Ministries. Again, just use the following as a general guideline. Your own situation may require a different approach or a modification of my suggestions.

Your Next Meeting

Once you have an interested group (even two or three people), the most important thing is to establish *goals* and a sense of direction. The group will flounder if it does not have a common purpose. Here is an agenda for an early meeting to begin formulating the group's goals.

Agenda

1. Prayer: Start with a Scripture reading on a peace and justice theme (e.g., Isaiah 58:3–11). Silent reflection. Prayer.

2. Introductions: Take time for each person to tell a little about themselves and why they are interested in a Peace and Justice Ministry.

3. Brainstorm Dreams and Visions: Ask people to respond to the question: "What ideas, hopes or dreams do I have for what our Peace and Justice Ministry could do and be?" Write the ideas on a large piece of paper that everyone can see. Encourage everyone to speak. Include your own ideas. Try not to get in a lot of discussion at this point, but just ask everyone to express their vision of the ministry.

4. Planning the Next Meeting: Ask who would like to meet with you to look at the "dreams and visions" and plan the next meeting based on them. Often peace and justice groups are "sparked" by one or two people who have a particularly strong commitment or sense of call around peace and justice issues. If such people are part of your group already and if they work well with others, then encourage them to be part of the planning committee. Decide on the date, place and time of the next full meeting and also of the planning committee's meeting.

5. Sign-Up Sheet: Add the names, addresses and phone numbers of any new people to your contact list.

6. Closing Prayer

7. Refreshments and Informal Discussion

Work of the Planning Committee

The task of the planning committee is to make the next meeting of the full group as meaningful as possible. People will fall away from the group if they don't feel that it's moving forward and accomplishing something. The first job of the planning committee, therefore, is to help the full group clarify its purpose and goals. Why are we meeting? What do we want to achieve?

The "dreams and visions" articulated in the last meeting of the full group are a good place to start. The hopes written on the paper express the participants' initial thinking about what they want the group to be and do. Can this list of ideas —now jotted down in no particular order—be divided into categories?

Four categories often emerge: (1) hopes for the internal life of our Ministry; (2) ideas for our relationship to the rest of the congregation; (3) thoughts for outreach beyond our local church; and (4) societal peace and justice issues in which participants have a particular interest or commitment.

Drawing from these ideas, the Planning Committee should be able to formulate a tentative list of goals and objectives for the full group's discussion and approval. For example, using the four categories above, the statement might look like the following:

Goals for Our Peace and Justice Ministry

Goals for the Internal Life of Our Ministry

1. To keep all our efforts rooted in prayer and the Gospel.
2. To grow in friendship and love for one another.
3. To encourage one another's gifts as peacemakers and justice-seekers.
4. To see any conflicts or disagreements among us, not as signs of failure, but as opportunities for growth and training in peacemaking.
5. To organize a self-education process so that together we learn more about specific peace and justice issues and how our faith relates to them.

Goals for Our Relationship to the Rest of the Congregation

1. To reach out with our concerns to the rest of the parish in an attitude of service.
2. To provide educational opportunities for parishioners around Christian faith and its relationship to peace and justice issues.
3. To design programs, activities and actions that parishioners can enter into as an expression of Christ's call to work for peace and justice.

32

Goals for Outreach Beyond Our Local Church

1. To cooperate in common education and action with other groups that share our commitment to faith-based peace and justice work.
2. To try to have an impact in the public realm—the policies, laws, and institutions of our society that promote violence and injustice.
3. To keep before us a special concern for the poor, asking how what we do affects or involves the poor.
4. To try to address the roots, and not just the fruits, of violence and injustice.

Goals Around Specific Peace and Justice Issues

1. To explore more deeply the peace and justice issues about which members of our Ministry feel especially strongly.
2. To set up a process to discern the specific peace and justice issues on which we should focus in our educational and action efforts.

Immediate Objectives for Our Ministry

1. During our next two meetings, we will try to discern which specific peace and justice issues we should address.
2. At the same time, we will set up a process to educate ourselves more deeply about these issues so that we gain clarity on how best to address them.

A statement of goals and objectives like this can be very helpful in giving a group a sense of direction. The planning committee may also want to draw up a tentative "Mission Statement" or "Statement of Purpose" for the Ministry, for example:

Draft Mission Statement

The purpose of the _____
Peace and Justice Ministry is to be a prayerful, loving group that acts for peace and justice and encourages our parish to deepen its education and action in peacemaking and justice-seeking.

At the next meeting of the full group, the planning committee can present its draft statements for discussion. Once the goals are approved, the group can begin to discuss what strategies or actions it can best develop to implement its goals.

Discernment of Issues

Sometimes a group will come together with a strong sense of the peace and justice issues that members want to work on. If there's already a high degree of consensus in your group about its focus, then you may not need a discernment process. You can skip this next section.

However, many groups begin with a general belief that their faith calls them to work for peace and justice but without having specific ideas for *particular* issues to which the group should give its energy. Or, the group may be pulled in several different directions, with some people caring about one set of questions, some about another. Other groups are formed at the pastor's request, but with very little guidance as to their expected focus. Such groups need to spend some time in discernment of issues.

The same God who cares about the poor and works for peace on earth also knows your group, loves every member of it, and has a special mission for it. The work of discernment is to discover together how God wants your group to use its members' gifts to work on behalf of God's Kingdom.

Obviously, not every group is called to the same issues or tasks. Each group has its unique set of gifts, skills, experiences and opportunities. Discernment asks: What are we to be and do as members of Christ's Body at this moment of history, in this congregation and locale, with the unique people who make up our group?

I know of no simple formula for answering this question. Each group needs to spend sufficient time in prayer, discussion, study and involvement until clarity emerges. At some point, the group will be able to say "Yes, this is our focus, at least for now." Members will share a sense of excitement and energy, a feeling of rightness, of "fit." As Frederick Buechner says,

"The place God calls you to is the place where your deep gladness and the world's deep hunger meet."[11]

Here are a dozen steps that groups might take to gain that clarity:

1. Pray: In all things, keep asking God to clarify the group's call.

2. Trust: Don't worry about seeing the *whole* plan. Be willing to take one step at a time.

3. Be flexible: Don't assume that the whole group must agree to focus on exactly the same concerns. If differences persist in the group, set up subcommittees so that members can work on the different issues to which they feel called.

4. Study Scripture: Reflect together on passages that touch especially on peace and justice. Ask how they might apply to us today. For example, what does Jesus' story of Lazarus and the rich man (Luke 16:19–31) say about our response to the poor and hungry in our own community and world? What would the compassionate Jesus do if he were a member of our Church and lived in this community?

5. Use a list of issues: Chapter 1 in this book lists over forty issues that a Peace and Justice Ministry might address. Read them over in the

---

[11] Frederick Buechner, *Wishful Thinking - A Theological ABC* (New York and San Francisco: HarperCollins, 1973).

36

group. See if any of them strike a bell.

6. Listen to outrage: Remember that the Bible gives, not a philosophical description of justice, but an expression of God's *outrage* at injustice. What injustices outrage members of your group? Homeless people having to live on the streets? Children dying of hunger? Destruction of the environment? How is human dignity being violated? How are the poor and the ecosystem being abused? Can your outrage connect with God's to give a sense of call?

7. Listen to one another's call: Are there individuals in the group who already have a sense of calling or a deep interest around certain topics. Might the issues that grip them also engage the group? Let them take some time to inform the group about what attracts them and why they feel strongly about it.

8. Brainstorm possible issues: In brainstorming, we write on a large piece of paper any ideas the group has for problems it might focus on. No criticism or discussion. Just jot them down as people articulate them. Then go through the list and ask whether any of the questions really "grab" people. If they do, look into them more deeply and decide how to work on them.

9. Note what other groups are doing: Does your denomination or its social action agency have a peace and justice project that your group would like to support? What problems are local or

37

national peace and justice groups currently addressing? (See Appendix 2 for the names and addresses of several national groups you can contact.)

10. *Use resource people:* Who in your local area are respected advocates for peace and justice? Invite them to meet with you to share their ideas. Draw upon the experience of people who have worked for peace and justice for a long time.

11. *Study:* Read, read, read. Peace and justice questions often are complex. Know as much as possible about the ones that interest you so that your choice of an issue to work on is an informed one. The magazines and newsletters of national peace and justice organizations are often the best source of information on this subject. (See Appendix 2.) Many excellent books also explain the issues and how to approach them. Learn about peace and justice conferences and workshops that you can attend to become better informed.

12. *Act:* Remember Dr. Martin Luther King's warning about "the paralysis of analysis." Many people begin to hear a call when they become *directly involved* with the poor, for example, by volunteering in a soup kitchen, building homes with Habitat for Humanity, demonstrating for civil rights or writing letters for Amnesty International on behalf of political prisoners. Since God is especially present with the poor and the oppressed, we can expect to hear God's call as we draw near to them.

38

Leadership

The first few meetings of your Peace and Justice Ministry may be led by the person or persons who initially called the group together. However, it is good for the group to choose its own leaders. (Because the word "leader" can imply one who takes full responsibility for the group or who is always "out front," it may be better to use a more democratic term like "group coordinator" or "facilitator." These terms imply a leader who helps or facilitates the group to do what *it* chooses to do, rather than just following what the "leader" says.)

Often it's good to have rotating leadership. This gives everyone a chance to learn facilitation skills. Also, with each member sharing in leadership, a common sense of responsibility for the group will emerge. Don't force people to be leaders, however, if they really feel their gifts lie elsewhere.

Some groups may want to organize themselves formally, with a chairperson, vice-chair, secretary and treasurer. Others have a more informal leadership style. In any case, as the group develops, it will want to add committees to carry out particular tasks so that no one person is bearing more than his or her fair share of the work.

Planning Meetings

Facilitators should hold a planning meeting prior to the group's regular meeting. This means that they arrive at the larger meeting with a proposed agenda, rather than with the attitude, "Well, what shall we do now?" But don't be rigid about the agenda. Allow other members to suggest changes or add new items so that they'll feel they have a stake in the meeting too.

A Standard Agenda

Naturally, a group has to be flexible about its agenda depending upon its needs and the members' interests. However, certain points seem important to cover in every meeting, especially when the group is just getting started. Having a standard agenda can reduce confusion and help give the group a sense of direction and movement.

Model Agenda

1. *Prayer:* It is so easy to slip into being just an "activist" group, forgetting our need to be rooted in God. We need to reach out actively for God's peace and guidance. Some groups name a "worship coordinator" to give thought to its prayer.

2. *Personal Sharing:* Members of the group need to get to know one another on a personal basis. The group will be strengthened as it builds personal links of understanding and affection. A simple way to do this is for the facilitator to ask, "Could we go around the group and briefly share something interesting or exciting that has happened in our lives since the last meeting?"

3. *Self-Education:* As a group is getting started, people are hungry for information and answers to their questions. Time in the meeting can be set aside regularly to discuss an informative book, article or video, to hear an outside speaker, or to discuss a specially-prepared talk by one of the group's own members. (Some groups appoint an "education coordinator," a member who regularly brings materials for the group's self-education.)

4. *Business:* This includes both matters carried over from the last meeting and new business. As the group develops, this section probably will take up the bulk of the meeting time.

It's helpful if each item of business can be stated as a *question* to be answered or a *problem* to be solved. The group's discussion can then focus concretely on possible *answers* or *solutions*. The goal is to reach a decision representing the group's best shot at answering the question or solving the problem. When agreement is reached, the facilitator states the group's decision and the secretary records it in the minutes. Clear decision-making enlivens meetings!

41

5. *Open time:* This is an opportunity for people to bring up announcements, concerns, questions and so forth, that did not fit in the rest of the agenda.

6. *Action:* This item may not be necessary in the early group meetings, where the focus is on self-education and program planning. But it is helpful later. It reminds the group not to get bogged down in internal discussions, but to take action for peace and justice.

7. *Evaluation of the meeting:* See the end of this chapter for how to do an evaluation.

8. *Date and place of next meeting.*

One and a half to two hours seems to be the ideal length for most meetings. Concise and productive meetings can keep interest peaked. Meetings that drag out and last several hours can sap the group rather than strengthen it.

Not everything that happens with a peace and justice ministry necessarily happens during its business meetings. A peace group at Philadelphia's First United Methodist Church, for example, has supper together before its regular meetings. This gives time for personal sharing and getting to know one another better. Members find that having a chance to visit during the meal means that they are freer to focus on the agenda during their business meeting.

Other groups get together outside of meetings for parties, potlucks, recreation, retreats and so forth. Again, this helps to build unity and bonds of friendship in the group.

Using Effective Group Process in Meetings

Jesus said, "Where two or three are gathered together in my name, there am I in the midst of them" (Matthew 18:20).

Because Jesus, the Prince of Peace, really **is** present with us, and because we want to follow his commandment to love one another, our groups can experience an unusual depth of unity, harmony and common purpose. However, we are also human beings with our own strong convictions, faults, and set ways of doing things. We do not always agree. In fact, we sometimes get into outright conflicts with one another. Personalities can clash. Styles of running meetings can be very different. People can have very diverse ideas of how best to work for peace and justice.

Some degree of conflict seems to be present in nearly every group interaction. (Even the early Church knew "no little dissention and debate"—Acts 15:2.) Such conflict is bad only if it is handled destructively. If handled creatively, it can be a prime ingredient of needed change and growth.

Common Sources of Conflict in Peace and Justice Groups

1. Difficulty agreeing on goals, priorities, what to do.

2. Group leaders not being skilled in running meetings.

3. Not planning meeting agendas ahead of time.

4. One person speaking too much, dominating discussion, not listening, interrupting, "hogging the show."

5. Others being passive, never speaking up.

6. Some people doing all the work, then feeling "burnt out" or resentful at those doing less.

7. Differences in theology or political philosophy.

8. Personality conflicts.

9. People who are negative, find something wrong in every proposal, "nitpick."

10. People with hidden agendas, who try to shift the focus of every discussion to their own pet ideas.

11. People who are dogmatic and defensive, making a last stand for their positions, even on minor issues, responding to contrary opinions as a personal attack.

12. People who have difficulty focusing upon the current discussion and seek to redirect it at inappropriate times with tangential comments.

Ways to Deal with Conflict

Reconciliation should be a key attitude among members of a peace and justice ministry. Any serious conflict between members should be worked through, and minor conflicts should be dealt with before they become major ones. We need to strive to be at peace with one another if we want to be peacemakers in the world. Here are some proven ideas for working together effectively:

1. Encourage people to take a *different view* of conflict and disagreement. It's not wrong, dangerous, un-Christian, or something to be avoided at all costs. It's inevitable and can produce creative problem-solving by looking at all sides of a question. Therefore, don't be thrown by differences of opinion. Encourage the expression of differences. Don't form cliques of the like-minded. Reach out to talk/listen to those with whom you disagree. The important thing is to listen respectfully to the differences and then work them through to a common approach.

2. Choose *leaders or coordinators* who have a positive attitude, are open to the ideas of others and good at facilitating meetings. A good facilitator keeps the group on the topic with charity and flexibility, gently encourages hesitant members to speak up, and "leans on" those who talk too much. He or she reminds the group of its goals, spreads responsibility, and encourages an open, accepting, warm climate for discussion. He or she is a person who's good at helping the group *decide* what it wants to do and then *to do* what it decides to do.

3. *Plan meetings* ahead of time so that the group meets with a proposed written agenda before it. But let the group add to or change the agenda so they "own" it.

4. *Spread out responsibility* so that one person is not doing all the work. Set up subcommittees. Encourage and call forth the talents and gifts of each member.

5. If someone's behavior is especially irritating, have the courage to speak to him or her about it frankly and lovingly *outside the meeting,* rather than just letting it go. If people change for the better, let them know how much it is appreciated.

6. Find ways to counter unproductive behavior *right in the meeting.* "Excuse me, Bob, but I don't think Mary had a chance to finish her sentence before you spoke up." "Before we hear

from someone who's spoken before, let's hear
from someone who hasn't."

7. Encourage an atmosphere of *loving affirmation*
of people and their ideas. Everyone should feel
accepted and listened to. Encourage everyone to
express their own feelings and opinions. Resist
the temptation to pounce critically on another's
idea, making them feel defensive or withdrawn.
Instead, try to say something good about the idea
before offering one's own opinion.

8. Encourage group members really to *listen* to
one another. If this isn't happening, ask people to
try repeating what the last person in the
discussion said before offering their own opinion.

9. Forget the idea that there are "good guys and
bad guys." Every person can back up their
perspective with their own thinking and
experience. Try to understand people's opinions
and why they hold them. Stay in dialogue with a
humble posture. Be open to the possibility that
new truth may emerge that no one saw when the
discussion began.

10. When people raise objections to ideas,
encourage them to turn their concerns into
proposals. "My concern would be resolved if
(give concrete proposal)."

11. If you're really having trouble with someone,
try the *three-step approach* found in the Bible

and other spiritual traditions: (a) Ask, "Am I at fault? Do I need to apologize and set things right?" (b) Go to the person with whom you're having difficulty and honestly but lovingly share what's bothering you. (c) If you can't work it out between yourselves, ask someone else to help you.

12. A sense of *humor* is always helpful!

Evaluation

Setting aside times for evaluation is an important way to keep a group fresh and forward-moving. Group members need times when they can air complaints about the group or make suggestions for improvement. If they do not get this opportunity and if their concerns get buried or bottled up, they may become discouraged and drop out. Many groups, therefore, make evaluation a regular part of each meeting's agenda.

A simple but effective format for evaluation is to have a large piece of paper divided into three columns. Put a plus sign (+) at the top of the first column, a minus sign (-) at the top of the second column and an arrow (→) atop the third.

The facilitator first asks people to express all the things they *like* about the way things have been going in the group. These positives are written in the plus column. (This is a very important first step. We need to remind ourselves of what we have done well, the good things we can build on. If we hear only criticisms, we can easily become discouraged.) The facilitator then writes in the minus column people's *criticisms* or feelings about things that could be improved. Finally, the facilitator asks people who have voiced dissatisfactions to say, if possible, *how* they think things could be improved. (This means that the group is not just left with criticisms, which could be a real "downer," but instead has a whole list of suggestions for improvement.)

A group's evaluation of its "Peace and Justice Film Festival" might look like the following:

Plus (+)	Minus (-)	Arrow (→)
●Good publicity ●Good attendance ●Tasty food ●Excellent film ●Reached new people	●Many new people came, but we did not get their names and addresses. ●People did not speak up in the large-group discussion after the meeting.	●Be sure to pass around a sign-up sheet the next time we have such an event. ●Next time, try dividing into small discussion groups.

At the end of such an evaluation, the group has a sense of what it is doing well, where people are dissatisfied and how things can be improved.

Chapter Four

How Your Group Can

Work for Peace and

Justice

Program Ideas

A group can "go under" if it has bad group process or inept leadership. But it also can fail if it is not accomplishing anything significant, if its members feel it is just spinning its wheels. Therefore, a peace and justice ministry needs to know how it can engage in meaningful programs of education and action around its concerns. This section will briefly describe some programs actually carried out by church-based peace and justice groups. Then it will outline several ways that your group might become involved.

Examples of Parish-Based Action for Peace and Justice

From the 1970s up to the present, hundreds of local churches and their peace and justice groups have worked for peace with justice in Central America. Many churches in the Southwest assisted refugees who came across the border from Mexico, fleeing persecution from the "death squads" and out-of-control military of Guatemala and El Salvador. In Philadelphia, the Quaker Peace Committee of Germantown Friends Meeting, like similar groups throughout the USA, became part of the "Sanctuary Movement." They sponsored Central American refugees, helped them find housing and work, and protested our government's support for the military regimes that caused their persecution. The Peace and Justice Ministry of my own parish, St. Vincent's, joined other church groups in establishing a "Sister Parish" relationship with a poor community in El Salvador. We also held nonviolent prayer vigils in front of our U.S. Senator's office, urging a change in American policy toward Central America. St. Williams parish, in Louisville, Kentucky, also became a Sanctuary church, sent delegations to El Salvador, and maintained a high profile in opposing the U.S.-driven "contra" war in Nicaragua. In addition, it's Service Committee set up the "New Directions Housing Corporation," started a neighborhood center, and managed a store that sells third world crafts while educating customers about relations between our country and poorer nations.

Note in these efforts the combination of charity or service (the Good Samaritan principle) with a striving for justice (the prophetic principle). Participants respond directly to refugees and others in dire need. Yet they also work to change the misguided government policies that did so much to create the need in the first place. Like the people by the roadside in Sister Joan Chittister's story in Chapter 1, they have not been satisfied just to heal the wounds of those who crashed into the boulder. They also have tried to remove the boulder from the road.

Other parish groups have focused on issues closer to home. The Peace and Justice Ministry of St. John the Evangelist Church in Bucks County, Pennsylvania has joined with other church groups

54

to form the Interfaith Housing Development Corporation, which provides habitation for low income people. Church members across the country volunteer with Habitat for Humanity, which builds and rehabilitates houses for the poor. Many parish peace and justice groups, like the one at St. Andrew's parish in Drexel Hill, Pennsylvania, reach out to the homeless by volunteering in shelters or distributing food to people living on the street. With the assistance of its Outreach Committee, more than a quarter of the members of St. Paul's Episcopal Church in Philadelphia have become involved in service and justice work. They cook meals for AIDS patients and at a homeless shelter, feed needy families in the parish hall and work to rehabilitate housing for low income people. An even higher proportion of the members of the ecumenical Church of the Savior in Washington, DC is involved in its service and justice ministries. All members commit themselves, not only to daily prayer and Bible study, but also to active involvement in one of the missions of the church. Focusing on the weak, the defenseless and the outcast, they have developed innovative, staffed programs around housing, health care, employment, refugees, the elderly, the homeless, children and international peace.

St. Mary's parish in Aberdeen, Washington not only has a lunch program that feeds 2,000 poor people a month, but its members also travelled to the State capitol to lobby for strong unemployment assistance in light of their county's 13.2% jobless rate. Catholics, Episcopalians and Lutherans come together in New York's East Brooklyn Congregations, which provided 2,300 homes for poor and moderate income people over the last eight years.

Parish peace and justice groups work on an enormous variety of issues. Members of the Peace and Justice Ministry of St. Charles Borromeo Church in Drexel Hill, Pennsylvania, were inspired by the U.S. Bishops' statement on domestic violence. To raise consciousness on the issue, they asked parishioners to wear white ribbons to show support for the statement and to take a unified stand rejecting violence against women. They also worked with teachers in the parish school to develop a peace and justice curriculum and have helped CCD students become involved in service projects. The Peace and Justice Ministry of Our Lady of Mt. Carmel in Doylestown, Pennsylvania, planted a peace garden on the grounds of the parish and organized Stations of the Cross peace marches to a local Naval Air Base. Given its locale's economic hardship and high unemployment, it also has joined with two nearby parishes, St. Andrew's and St. John the Evangelist, to create "Management in Transition," a program that puts together jobs and job-seekers. The African American Leadership Ministry, a justice group in my parish, gives workshops on dismantling racism and distributes a leaflet it wrote called "12 Things You Can Do to Combat Racism." Across the street, the Faith Chapel Church of God in

Christ leads marches against racism and provides literacy training for neighbors who can't read or write.

Corpus Christi Parish, in Rochester, New York, is not only a sanctuary church, but also staffs a shelter for the homeless, a day care center for low income families, a health clinic in a poor part of the city, a hospice for the dying, a house for homeless pregnant teenagers, and a restaurant where ex-convicts, released from a local prison, can find work, training, and a new lease on life. They see these ministries as "homeless prevention projects." Since ecology is also a justice issue, the Baptist Church of the Valley, in San Ramon, California was built to be heated by solar energy. It uses 75 percent less energy than a comparable church that has to rely on nonrenewal resources like coal, oil or gas.

Over a dozen parish peace and justice groups in the Philadelphia Archdiocese, and many more nationwide, have participated in "Children and Families First." This national campaign seeks to educate parishioners and the public about the needs of the family and to support national legislation that helps families protect their children's lives. In the low income community in Phoenix, Arizona, where St. Catherine's Parish is located, gangs ruled the streets and drive-by shootings were terrorizing children and families. Working with other community leaders, parishioners conceived a plan to take back their neighborhood and develop a crime-free, drug-free community. Drive-by shootings were reduced and

St. Catherine's is beginning to work with other churches on wider issues of equity and justice.

Like many peace and justice ministries, the Pax Christi group of St. Joseph's Church in Shreveport focuses on peace and disarmament. They have demonstrated and prayed for peace at Barksdale Air Force Base, the second largest SAC base in the country, and outside the offices of their member of Congress. At the end of the Persian Gulf war, the Peace and Justice Commission of Rock Island's St. Joseph's parish held an ecumenical gathering to ask forgiveness for all the death and destruction the war caused.

As you can see, these efforts range from the very simple to the nearly heroic. In some of the churches, peace and justice work has become so pervasive that the whole congregation has become a peace and justice *church*—not a bad goal for a peace and justice *ministry*. I have given only a few examples of hundreds that could be mentioned in which Christians whose backgrounds are Presbyterian, Disciples, Mennonite, Brethren, UCC, AME, Christian Reformed, Seventh Day Adventist, Moravian, Unitarian and other denominations too numerous to mention are engaged in significant work for peace and justice.

How to Address an Issue— An Illustration: Hunger

A justice orientation implies trying to address the roots of social problems, not just their fruits. It means not only helping the victims of boulder crashes, but removing boulders. A number of the ministries mentioned above successfully combine a compassionate response to human need with a concern for changing the values, policies, laws or institutions that create the need in the first place.

As this book is being written, millions of people are facing starvation in Africa, with hundreds of thousands already dead. Around the world, 40,000 children die *each day* from malnutrition and related diseases.[12] In our own country, few people starve, yet many lack the nutrients necessary for growth and good health. According to the *Scientific American,* the number of hungry people in our country is an astounding twelve million children and eight million adults.[13]

How might a parish peace and justice group take up the issue of hunger in a way that holds together compassion and justice?

1. Hunger and Compassion

"I was hungry, and you fed me," Jesus said. Responding to Jesus, the group might begin by enabling people to volunteer at a homeless shelter or soup kitchen, as many church members

---

[12] Bread for the World, *Fact Sheet on Childhood Hunger and Poverty* (Washington, DC: Bread for the World, undated).

[13] J. Larry Brown, "Hunger in the U.S.," *Scientific American,* February 1987, pp. 37ff. Although this article was written in 1987, its basic statistics about hunger are still valid today.

around the country have done. If the church is located in or near a poor area, it might consider setting up its own soup kitchen, food cupboard, thrift shop or other program to directly aid the needy.

A Catholic parish in Philadelphia asks its members, when shopping, to buy a little extra for the poor and then to bring the food to Sunday Mass. At the Presentation of Gifts, just before Communion, the children of the parish bring baskets full of food down the aisle and place them on the altar as a vivid symbol of our responsibility to the hungry.

To respond to hunger overseas, the Peace and Justice Ministry might have special educational programs for the parish, with speakers or films from a relief and development agency like Catholic Social Services, Church World Service, or World Vision. Then it could organize special fund-raising drives, perhaps using a vehicle like "Operation Rice Bowl," which enables families to put aside money regularly for the poor and hungry.

2. Hunger and Justice

Hunger should not exist in the U.S., one of the richest countries in the world. According to the *Scientific American* article mentioned above, hunger in the U.S. was virtually eliminated in the 1970s. The blight returned because of Federal Government cut-backs in such programs as school lunches and breakfasts, food stamps, and nutrition for infants, pregnant women and the elderly. For example, from 1982–85, cutbacks caused one million children to be dropped from the school lunch program and 400,000 from the school breakfast program.[14] The vivid message is that the hungry can be fed, not only by soup kitchens, but by governmental policies and programs that respond effectively to their needs. To create and sustain such programs is the work of justice.

One of the most effective ways that Peace and Justice Ministries can work for justice-oriented hunger-prevention programs both in this country and abroad is through the national Christian organization, "Bread for the World" (see Appendix 2 for address). BFW is a Christian lobby that brings together literally tens of thousands of Protestants, Catholics and Evangelicals in sophisticated campaigns to educate the public and influence Congress to adopt policies and pass laws to eradicate hunger at home and overseas. BFW's 45,000 "lobbyist members" receive a monthly newsletter that alerts them when members of Congress need to be contacted. They also get special educational materials about the root causes of hunger. They form "Quickline" telephone networks to respond to fast-moving events in Washington. During elections, they do voter-registration campaigns and urge candidates to commit themselves on hunger policies. They come together in groups,

[14] Brown, "Hunger in the U.S.," p. 41.

61

often in local churches, to worship, study and act for the elimination of hunger.

To take a justice approach to the issue of hunger, therefore, a local Peace and Justice Ministry could contact BFW, get its materials, and start a parish program based on its approach.

This same combination of compassion and justice can be applied to issues like housing, medical care, abortion, race relations, homelessness, ecology, human rights and many others. Whatever issue or issues your Ministry chooses, therefore, keep searching for how to address the roots of the problem as well as how to respond to the fruits.

Some Methods of Education and Action

Regardless of the issue or issues your ministry chooses, a wide variety of effective methods are available for getting your message across. Here are some of these methods, grouped under eight focus areas.

1. Peace and Justice in Your Members' Families

• *Reading:* Buy books for your children that reflect peace and justice themes and recount the lives of people—like Martin Luther King, Dorothy Day, Cesar Chavez, Harriet Tubman—

who have led the struggle to build a better world. Some of the organizations listed in Appendix 2 can provide lists of age-appropriate readings.

• *Ideas for Parents:* Write Jim and Kathy McGinnis for their books and materials on "Parenting for Peace and Justice" (Institute for Peace and Justice, 4144 Lindell Blvd. #124, St. Louis, MO 63108). Perhaps no one has done more than this Catholic couple to come up with creative suggestions for incorporating peace, justice and nonviolence into family life.

• *Volunteer Opportunities:* Volunteering, for example, to serve meals at a soup kitchen, can be a wonderful way to expose the whole family, including children, to the realities of poverty and hunger. Parents can encourage teenagers to volunteer in the many church-based programs designed especially to educate young people about peace, justice and service to the needy.

2. Internal Education for Your Peace and Justice Ministry

• *Self-Education:* Have "self-education" as a regular agenda item for your meetings. Use the time to discuss a book or article or view an informative video. Name one of your own members to be your Education Coordinator. Give him or her the responsibility of bringing to the group the best recent information on peace and justice issues and concerns.

● *Magazine subscriptions:* Encourage everyone in your group to subscribe to at least one magazine that deals regularly with peace and justice issues. Two excellent magazines that focus consistently on these issues from a faith perspective are *The Other Side* (300 W. Apsley St., Philadelphia, PA 19144) and *Sojourners* (2401 15th St., NW, Washington, DC 20077–3815). If finances are a problem, subscribe as a group and pass the magazines around among the members.

● *Membership in organizations:* Encourage members to join local and national peace and justice organizations. (See Appendix 2 for suggestions.) These organizations have trained, experienced staff who make it their business to stay up-to-date. Receiving their newsletters and other literature is one of the best ways to become informed about complex issues and to get ideas on how best to act.

● *Books:* The national organizations in Appendix 2 have lists of the best books on peace and justice.

● *Teaching:* Act on the premise that the best learning comes through teaching. Suggest that a member of your ministry study an issue of special interest to the group and make a report on it. Having to prepare a talk is a great way to learn a subject thoroughly.

• *Learn Through Action:* Mother Teresa says that we can see Christ in the slums, in the broken bodies of the forgotten poor. Have your group spend time helping at a soup kitchen or shelter for the homeless. Look for Christ in the poor. When you return, reflect together on Matthew 25:31–46.

3. Education for the Local Congregation

• *Bulletin:* Put notices and information about your concerns or up-coming events in the Sunday bulletin.

• *Worship Services:* Work with your minister or liturgy committee to explore how to introduce peace and justice themes into worship services through sermons, prayers, music and Bible selections. Pray for governments, for enemies, for peace and justice in the world.

• *Evening Meeting:* Organize and publicize an evening meeting with a good speaker, film or video. Have an "information night" and invite a speaker from Amnesty International, Pax Christi or Bread for the World to describe their organization's work and how parishioners can become involved. (Good speakers often can be located through local peace and justice organizations.)

• *Literature:* Set up a literature table or bulletin board in the church with your leaflets, posters, books and announcements of events.

• *Retreats:* Have a retreat focusing on the spirituality of peace and justice.

• *Actions:* Give opportunities for members of the congregation to participate in actions for peace and justice, such as prayer vigils, processions, nonviolent demonstrations. People often learn by doing as much as by discussing.

• *Petitions:* Gather signatures on a petition concerning a peace or justice issue.

• *Prayer Service:* Organize a special prayer service around a current peace or justice issue.

• *Bible Study:* Offer to organize a Church Bible study to explore what Scripture teaches about peace and justice. (See Appendix 1 for such a Bible study.)

• *Special Events:* Use special times—Martin Luther King's birthday, Black History Month, Earth Day, Peace Sunday, International Human Rights Day. etc.—as an opportunity to get your message out through literature, sermons, speakers, workshops.

• *Relations With Your Pastor:* Keep your minister informed about your group's work and

regularly send him or her articles and other
information on your concerns.

• *Network With Other Parish Groups:* Don't
isolate your group. Take part in the general work
of the parish. The most successful ministries are
those that interact regularly with other parish
groups, for example, suggesting prayers for peace
to the Liturgy Committee, proposing speakers for
adult class to the Religious Education Committee,
doing joint actions with the Pro-Life Group. Keep
explaining the spiritual roots of your commitment
to peace and justice.

4. Peace and Justice Education in the Broader Community

• *Meetings:* Hold a broadly-advertised public
meeting at your Church addressed by a well-
known speaker on a current issue.

• *Ecumenical Services:* Co-sponsor a special
worship service on a peace or justice theme with
other congregations.

• *Displays:* Many communities have town fairs
with booths set up to display handicrafts, pottery
and artwork. Ask to set up a booth stocked with
peace and justice literature, bumper stickers,
petitions, posters, buttons, T-shirts.

• *Be Creative!* In Amityville, New York,
members of the Simpson United Methodist

Church designed a puppet show called "Puppets
for Peace" and presented it at fairs and
conferences. An ecumenical group of representatives from several Protestant and Catholic
Churches in Winona, Minnesota, got their town's
Mayor to declare a "Focus on Peace Week."

5. Peace and Justice Education in the Broader Church

• *Encourage Denominational Action:* Find out
what your own Church is doing at the local or
national level. Do they have staff or offices doing
education and action on peace and justice? Are
they trying to help local Churches become better
informed and more active? If your Church is not
yet active on these questions, find ways to
encourage them to make faith-based peace and
justice a priority. For example, you might set up
a literature display at an annual meeting and
engage other participants in discussion.

• *Schools and Colleges:* How do your Church-
related educational institutions reflect the mind of
Christ on questions of peace and justice? Do
students and faculty belong to peace and justice
groups? Does the school have speakers on issues
such as nonviolence, the poor, ecology, etc.?
Encourage them to include peace and justice
issues in their classes. Point out that some
colleges now offer courses and even degrees in
peace and justice studies.

6. Spreading the Message Through the Mass Media

• Work wherever possible to get *newspapers, radio and television* to carry editorials, articles, interviews, films on peace and justice issues. This is a way your message can reach hundreds of thousands of people.

• Don't overlook *letters to the editor* of your local newspaper. Readership surveys show that these are among the best-read features. Write concise, double-spaced, type-written letters on timely topics.

• Whenever your group has an event (e.g., a speaker), assign one of your members to write a *press release* on it and circulate it to the local media.

• If your speaker is well-known and/or particularly articulate and well informed, try to get him or her interviewed on a radio *talk show* or by a news reporter or columnist.

• If you learn of a particularly good film on a peace and justice topic, approach the *program director* of your local TV station and ask if they would be willing to broadcast it.

• Phone local radio *call-in shows* and voice your views.

7. Political Action

• Provide your group with the *phone numbers and addresses* of your Representatives and Senators. Encourage calls, letters and visits to these Congressional leaders when important legislative issues are coming up.

• Find out where your *Members of Congress* stand on peace and justice issues. Support those who take a strong position.

• Take a Church delegation to *see your representatives* when they are home for holidays or recesses. Ask them where they stand on the issues. Get specifics. Aim to get commitments, e.g., to introduce or vote for a specific piece of legislation. Make clear that your group wants to be represented by someone who supports the issues you feel are vital.

• Get on the mailing list of one of the national *religious lobbies* that work for peace and justice. (See "Network" in Appendix 2.) Use their material to lobby for particular legislation that holds promise of promoting peace with justice.

8. Prayerful Nonviolent Public Witnessing

• Study up on Christian nonviolent action as a method of working for peace and justice. Read, for example:

Nonviolence: A Christian Interpretation by William Robert Miller (New York: Shocken Books, 1972).

Nonviolence: The Invincible Weapon? by Ronald J. Sider (Dallas: Word Publishing, 1989).

Disarming the Heart: Toward a Vow of Nonviolence by John Dear, SJ (New York: Paulist Press, 1987).

• Contact local organizations that organize nonviolent demonstrations around peace and justice issues. See if your group would feel comfortable being involved in one of their actions.

• After due preparation and training, have your group organize its own prayerful public witness, e.g., at a toxic waste site where negotiations have failed to achieve a clean-up.

• Support and encourage your members' involvement in national demonstrations for peace and justice, e.g., rallies at our nation's Capitol to support housing for the poor.

When we get to heaven, Jesus will ask, "Did you live your life like I lived mine? Let me see your hands. Are they worn out from feeding the poor? Are your feet worn out from visiting the prisoners? Does your heart look anything like mine—broken open for others? Well, then, we must be part of the same family. Welcome home." (Fr. Jim Callan, pastor of Corpus Christi Church, Rochester, New York, at a parish peace and justice conference, Philadelphia, PA, November 1990).

Supplementary

Materials

Resources for Study, Worship, Reflection and Training

A Scripture Study on Social Justice

Many Christians are not fully aware of the Bible's profound teaching on social justice. Even those who are familiar with this teaching can find in Scripture study a new encounter with the God of living care whose abhorrence of injustice throbs in the words of the Bible. Here is a suggestion for a Bible study on justice for your group. Note that the passages cited are only a few of the hundreds in the Bible that address social justice. (A similar Scripture study can be done on peace.)

1. Have everyone bring a Bible to the study. It's fine if people have different translations. The variations sometimes shed new light on familiar passages.

2. Say that in our study we will be seeking the answers to six questions about justice. Our goal is to come to a deeper awareness of how the God we worship regards justice and injustice and how this understanding relates to our own life and mission.

3. Read the first of the six questions below. Then go around the circle and have members of the group read out loud the Bible passages listed under the question. Then discuss the question: "What do these passages say about God's attitude toward justice and injustice?"

4. Read the next of the six questions and go through the same process as above. If you need a question or comment to stimulate discussion, see those in parenthesis after the Bible quotes.

5. After the group has read all the questions and the associated Scripture passages, discuss the questions: "What are the implications for us of what we've heard? How do these passages apply to us in this church, this neighborhood, this country, this world?"

The Six Questions and Bible Passages

1. *What is God's attitude toward justice and injustice?*

- Leviticus 19:9–18
- Psalms 11:7; 89:15; 96:11–13; 99:3–5
- Isaiah 42:1–7; 61:8
- Jeremiah 9:22–23
- Amos 5:21–24

(Note what the Lord loves and hates.)

2. *How does God feel about the poor and the oppressed?*

- Exodus 22:20–26
- Psalms 9:8–13; 113:4–9
- Proverbs 19:17
- Matthew 25:31–46
- Luke 16:19–31

(How do your feelings about the poor and the oppressed compare with Gods?)

3. *How does God look upon oppressors, fomenters of injustice?*

- Psalms 82:1–5
- Proverbs 11:1; 14:31
- Isaiah 1:11–17; 3:14–15; 5:7–8, 20–23; 10:1–4
- Jeremiah 5:26–29; 22:13–17
- Ezekiel 16:49–50; 45:9
- Amos 2:6–8; 5:7–15
- Malachi 3:5
- Matthew 23:23–24
- Mark 12:38–40

(Can it be said that God is outraged at those who oppress others? What are your feelings toward oppressors?)

4. *Does God act to overcome injustice and oppression?*

- Psalms 12:6; 14:6; 103:6; 140:13–14; 146:5–9
- Proverbs 22:22–23
- Jeremiah 20:13
- Luke 4:18–19

(Note how Scripture portrays God as protecting the poor and fighting on the side of the oppressed? Is this the way we act? Why or why not?)

5. *How does God want us to act to overcome injustice?*

- Exodus 23:1–9
- Deuteronomy 10:12–19; 16:19–20
- Psalms 112:4–10
- Proverbs 21:13; 31:8–9
- Isaiah 1:16–17
- Jeremiah 7:4–7; 9:22–23; 22:3
- Micah 6:6–8
- Zechariah 7:9–10
- Matthew 5:43–48
- Luke 10:29–37
- 1 John 3:16–18

(Does God ask us to join in the struggle for love and justice? How?)

6. *How does God help us to fight injustice and oppression?*

- Psalms 11:5–7; 41:2–4; 97:10–12; 140:13–14
- Isaiah 58:6–11
- Matthew 5:3–12

(Did you ever think that fighting against injustice would be a way to be happy, healed and blessed? That it would be a way to be guided and strengthened by God?)

Reflection on a Biblical Passage

Instead of looking at *many* verses of Scripture, select one portion that is especially meaningful for peace or justice. Read these verses aloud while the rest of the group reflects prayerfully on their meaning. Have a period of quiet. Then spend some time sharing with one another what the passage is saying to each of you, how it relates to this time and place. Close by praying for one another and for God's guidance on how you can live out the implications of the passage in your daily lives.

Searching for Inner Peace

Read the passage in John 14:27 where Jesus says, "My peace I leave with you, my peace I give to you." Have members of the group reflect on how they find inner peace. Perhaps for

one it comes from being outdoors in nature, for
another through prayer, for someone else by
talking to a trusted friend. Have people share
these examples with the group. Then pray, asking
Jesus' presence to be with you during your
meeting.

Hold a Retreat to Grow
in Nonviolence

Order from Pax Christi (see address in
Appendix 2) the retreat manual, *Following the
Nonviolent Jesus*. This retreat brings together the
teachings of Jesus, Dorothy Day, Martin Luther
King, Jr. and Mohandas Gandhi, to provide an
opportunity to learn about and reflect on
nonviolence. Participants will get the most from
the retreat if they read ahead of time other brief
readings that can be ordered from Pax Christi,
such as *Martin Luther King: The Dream of a Just
Community, Gandhi the Peacemaker, Nonviolence
in the Christian Tradition, Love Your Enemies,
Active Nonviolence: A Way of Personal Peace*,
and *A Nonviolent Lifestyle*.

Do Your Own Nonviolence
Training

Nothing teaches nonviolence quite so
quickly as participation in an actual training
session in nonviolence. My wife and I did a video

and training manual to help groups do such training on their own. The package is called *The Practice of Peace: A Manual and Video for Nonviolence Training*. It shows groups how to do nonviolence training without having to rely on outside experts or people with previous experience in nonviolence. It can be ordered for $24.50 from the Sojourners Community, 2401 15th St., NW, Washington, DC 20077-3815.

National Peace, Justice and Ecology Organizations

In the United States, the citizens' movement for peace, justice and care for the environment is extremely widespread. Concerned people have organized literally thousands of groups at the local, state and national levels. Obviously, I cannot list all of them. Therefore, I have chosen seven longstanding national organizations with excellent reputations whose staffs are eager to help people work effectively for a more just, peaceful and ecologically sound world.

All of these organizations provide extensive lists of literature, films and videos, workshop and conference opportunities, etc. to help people become better informed. All of them suggest concrete and practical action that people can take to build a better world. Getting on the mailing lists of such organizations is one of the best ways that your parish Peace and Justice Ministry can keep up to date on current issues and learn when and how to act. Some of their material is free, others require a payment or membership fee. These costs are quite modest, considering what you receive. However, if expense is a factor, you can join the organization as a group and pass the materials around among your members.

If you want to learn about *other* peace, justice and ecology groups not listed here, your local library may be able to help. Also, the Quakers have a well-deserved reputation for being on the cutting edge of peace and social action. Their national service and social action organization is the American Friends Service Committee, 1501 Cherry Street, Philadelphia, PA 19102–1479 (telephone: 215–241–7000). If you want information on other local, state or national groups, write or phone them at their national office or at one of their several regional offices around the country.

The Organizations

Bread for the World
802 Rhode Island Ave., NE
Washington, DC 20018.
Telephone: 202–269–0200.

See the description of BFW in Chapter 4 of this book. BFW is the only Christian citizen's lobby that focuses solely on how to end hunger. It brings together tens of thousands of Protestants, Catholics and Evangelicals to lift up the needs of hungry people—here and abroad—to our national leaders in Washington. Motivated and nurtured by faith, these citizens work for national policies that will meet the immediate needs of hungry people and address those problems and situations which leave people hungry in the first place. Annual memberships are $25 or whatever a person can afford. Group as well as individual memberships are possible.

Fellowship of Reconciliation
Box 271, Nyack, NY 10960.
Telephone: 914–358–4601.

Founded at the end of World War I, the interfaith FOR is one of the oldest pacifist organizations in the U.S. It publishes the highly informative, monthly *Fellowship* magazine plus an enormous variety of books, pamphlets, audio-visuals and other materials on numerous peace and justice issues. It also sells cards, notes and gifts with peace and justice motifs. It is one of the world's pioneers in the application of nonviolence to peacemaking and social change. Membership is free to those who sign FOR's statement of purpose. Subscriptions to the magazine are $15 per year.

Friends Committee on National Legislation
245 Second St., NE
Washington, DC 20002.
Telephone: 202–547–6000.

FCNL is a Quaker lobby and information center that works to influence Congress and the White House on a broad range of national and international peace and justice concerns. It is one of the oldest faith-based lobbies in Washington and has an outstanding reputation for integrity and an ethical treatment of the issues. Its monthly newsletter, which goes to 10,000 Quaker and non-Quaker subscribers, covers a great many critical issues. It always contains practical suggestions for how to work for legislative or policy changes. Interested people can receive the newsletter for a donation of $25 or more.

Friends of the Earth
218 D Street, SE
Washington, DC 20003.
Telephone: 202–544–2600.

The U.S. has over 2,000 local, state and national environmental and conservation groups. It's impossible to list all of them, so I've chosen FOE as a global, non-profit advocacy organization dedicated to protecting the planet and its people. It helps its 50,000 members work on critical issues such as preventing further depletion of the earth's ozone layer, preventing and cleaning up chemical spills, combatting pollution of the atmosphere and water and laying the basis for sustainable development. For annual dues of $25, members receive a monthly magazine with in-depth articles on environmental questions and action suggestions. Much attention is focused on urging Congress and the Executive Branch to adopt the laws and policies that will support, rather than destroy, our environment. The magazine even has a "Kids Page for Young Activists" with projects for young people.

Network
806 Rhode Island Ave., NE
Washington, DC 20018.
Telephone: 202–526–4070.

Network is a national Catholic social
justice lobby rooted in Catholic social teaching
and Gospel values. Since 1971, it has been
lobbying Congress to enact laws providing
economic justice for the poor, protecting human
rights at home and abroad, promoting
disarmament and ensuring world peace. Its 10,000
members pay $30 annual dues ($15 low income)
and put their faith into action by advocating for
justice in legislation and by pushing for public
policies that address the systemic causes of
poverty and injustice. Network keeps its members
well informed on a wide array of crucial issues
through a bi-monthly newsletter, background
papers with in-depth treatment of issues, topical
leaflets, action alerts and information on Members
of Congress' voting records. It has an impressive
record of legislative achievement. You need not
be Catholic to join Network.

Pax Christi USA
348 East Tenth St.
Erie, PA 16503–1110.
Telephone: 814–453–4955.

"Pax Christi" means "the peace of Christ."
Pax Christi USA is a national Catholic organization that works for peace and justice by
exploring the ideal of Christian nonviolence and

87

by striving to apply it to personal life and to the structures of society. Its international parent body is headed by a Catholic Cardinal while its U.S. section has over 90 Catholic Bishops and 390 Catholic religious communities as members and corporate sponsors.

It supports 250 local groups and 35 campus groups around the U.S. and has thousands of individual members who pay its $20 annual membership dues. Members receive a quarterly magazine and other excellent material on peace and justice issues, always written from a prayerful, Gospel viewpoint and often suggesting actions that can be taken to promote peace and justice. Most Pax Christi materials reflect a Catholic point of view (e.g., a pamphlet on "Mary, Wellspring of Peace"), but many non-Catholics find its resources inspiring and helpful. However, although I do not have space to list them here, most other major denominations also have their own peace and justice offices and organizations.

Sojourners
2401 15th Street, NW
Washington, DC 20009.
Telephone: 202–328–8842.

Sojourners is an ecumenical Christian community in our nation's Capitol whose vocation is to serve and nurture Christians working for spiritual and social transformation. For a base commitment of $30, those who "join the sojourn" receive *Sojourners* magazine (always packed with informative articles), advance notice of public actions for peace and justice, support for local peace and justice projects and a periodic catalog of books, music, videos, audiotapes and study guides on many topics, all from a deeply Christian point of view.

BROWN-ROA
Resources and Supplements

Home Sweet Home (video)

The Many Faces of Jesus (video)

Citizens of the Kingdom (video)

Being a Catholic Christian Today (video)

Justice: Catholic Faith at Work in the World

Choose Life!

Avoiding Burnout

The Ministry Explosion

Leading Prayer

Call
1–800–922–7696

for these and other resources

 **BROWN-ROA**
A Division of Wm. C. Brown Communications, Inc.